URBAN
Nature

URBAN Nature

Catherine Baker

Collins

CONTENTS

Be a city nature-spotter.................2

Chapter 1 Mammals 4

City mammals around the world 14

Chapter 2 Birds 16

The crow family 24

Chapter 3 Minibeasts..................26

Minibeasts and not-so-mini beasts.......36

Chapter 4 Plants 38

Amazing city nature projects 46

Chapter 5 Hidden nature...............48

Chapter 6 Inviting nature in 58

Glossary 68

About the author 70

Book chat 72

BONUS

BE A CITY NATURE-SPOTTER

Wherever you live, you can spot nature on your own doorstep. You just need to know where to look!

LOOK UP

Look up when you're outside. Here are some of the amazing natural sights you might see.

LOOK DOWN

Find a quiet spot and crouch down to look for the tiniest plants and animals. You might see these even on a city street.

CHAPTER 1
MAMMALS

What's the best place to spot wild animals? The countryside? Not necessarily!

Curiously, it's sometimes easier to spot animals in the city. That's because city animals are more used to humans, and less likely to run away when they see you!

Lots of amazing animals live in towns and cities, from the tiniest insects to larger **urban** mammals like foxes.

I'm not shy!

Human and squirrel – two mammals together!

Mammals are animals that have hair or fur and feed their babies with milk. The most obvious mammals living in the city are us humans! But you'll find lots of other mammals happily sharing this space with us.

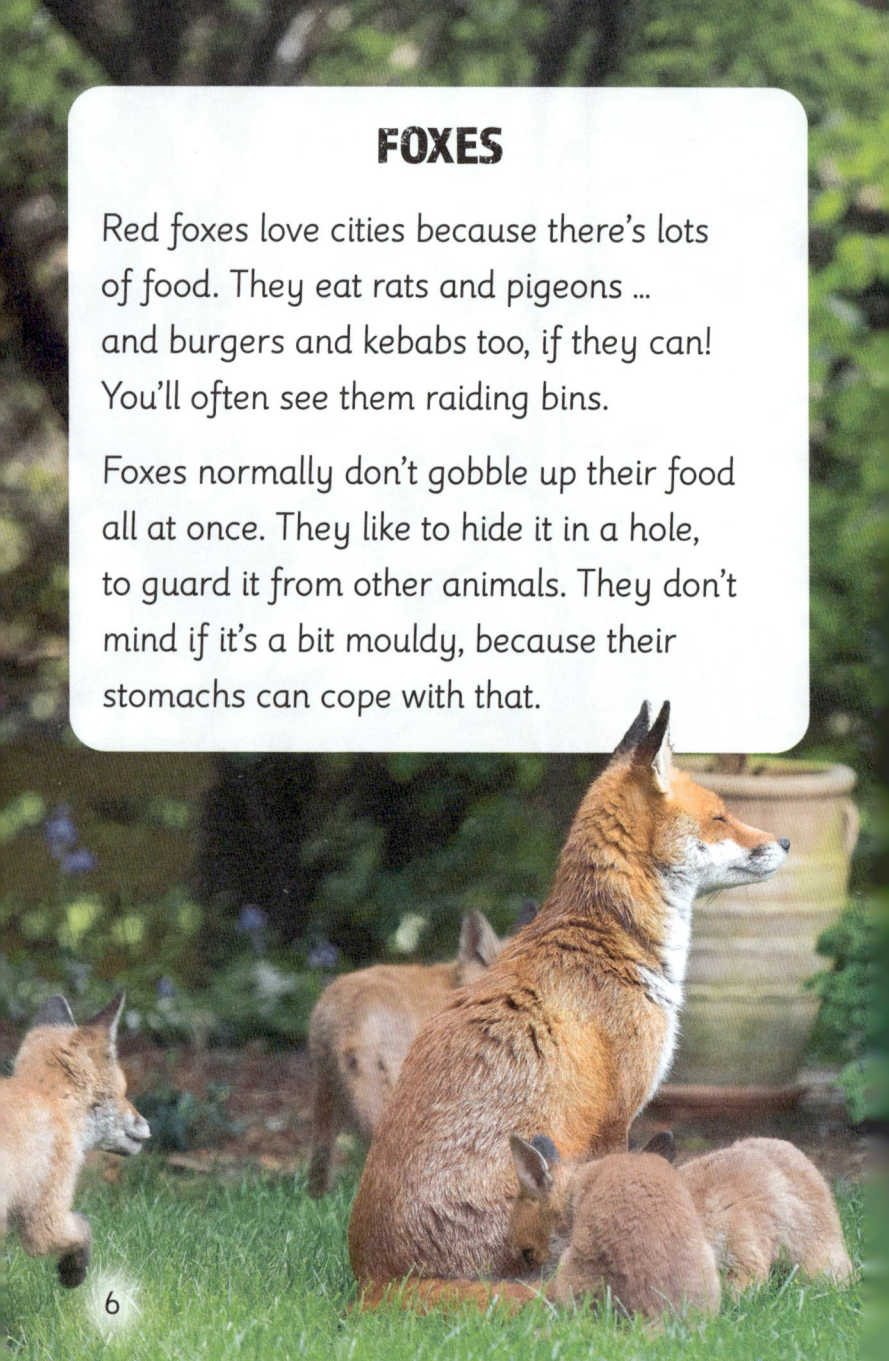

FOXES

Red foxes love cities because there's lots of food. They eat rats and pigeons ... and burgers and kebabs too, if they can! You'll often see them raiding bins.

Foxes normally don't gobble up their food all at once. They like to hide it in a hole, to guard it from other animals. They don't mind if it's a bit mouldy, because their stomachs can cope with that.

Foxes live in underground dens called earths. In the city, they dig earths under sheds, or alongside railways. Fox cubs are born in these dens.

Fox fact!
Some urban foxes live in unusual places. While building a London skyscraper called The Shard, workers found a fox living on the seventy-second floor! It survived by eating food they left behind.

SQUIRRELS

Grey squirrels are curious, clever and agile. You'll often spot them in city parks and gardens, or even running daringly along a cable!

Squirrels use their long tails to balance as they run and jump. They also use them to communicate! If you see a squirrel flicking its tail, it's probably telling other squirrels who's boss.

Squirrel fact!

Grey squirrels make nests called dreys, high up in trees. They use sticks, leaves and bark. Dreys look like birds' nests, but messier!

If you don't believe squirrels are intelligent, just watch one taking seeds from a bird feeder. They can hang precariously upside down and grab a sneaky pawful of seeds through the wires!

RATS

There are about 80 million rats in the UK, and many live in towns and cities.

Rats are usually most active at dawn or dusk. However, you might see one in daylight if it is hungry. Like foxes, rats enjoy raiding bins!

Rats are brilliant problem-solvers when it comes to finding food. Because of their powerful sense of smell, they can easily sniff food out.

Rat fact!

Rats' teeth never stop growing. They keep chomping to stop their teeth getting too big.

Once rats have smelt food, they have the skills to get close to it. Their sharp, strong teeth can nibble through hard materials, like wood and metal, to reach food.

They can even squeeze into buildings through holes as small as a ten pence coin!

BONUS CITY MAMMALS AROUND THE WORLD

Lots of black bears live in the US, and they sometimes come into towns looking for food.

Monkeys like this live in the city of Florianópolis, Brazil.

Wild deer wander the streets of Nara, Japan.

If you visit South Africa, you might see baboons in the cities!

CHAPTER 2
BIRDS

When birds look down at your city or town from the sky, what do they see? Not a grey sea of concrete, but a varied landscape full of opportunities waiting to be seized! Tall buildings might look like cliffs to nest on. Parks and gardens are full of trees that give food and shelter. Rivers and canals guarantee plenty of food for fish-eating birds, too.

The city of Manchester from the air

Some birds, like pigeons and sparrows, live in the city all year round. Others only fly over briefly, on their way to somewhere else. But if you look up, you're almost certain to be rewarded by the sight of a bird!

PIGEONS

It is easy to overlook pigeons, because we see them all the time. But actually, pigeons are intelligent, interesting, and also beautiful. If you look closely, you'll notice they're not just drab and grey. Their neck feathers shimmer with metallic greens, bronzes and purples.

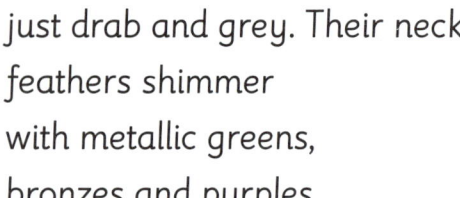

Pigeon fact!
Pigeons are so clever that they can recognise their own reflections in a mirror or puddle! Most animals can't do this.

Pigeons are also good parents. Mothers and fathers share the job of looking after their chicks (which are called squabs). They take turns to keep the unhatched eggs warm. When the squabs are hatched, both mother and father can produce a liquid called "crop milk". This is full of fat and **nutrients**, and ideal for feeding the squabs.

Most birds only lay eggs once or twice a year, but pigeons in cities can keep on laying eggs all year round. That's because lots of food is available for them.

Pigeons like to nest high up on buildings. Their nests are even messier than squirrel dreys!

SPARROWS

House sparrows have been living close to us humans for centuries. They like to eat our food scraps, and nest in holes in our buildings. They usually don't find humans very scary, so it's easy to watch them hopping about.

Adult sparrows are mostly vegetarian – they eat grains and seeds. However, they feed insects to their chicks.

Which chick will get the insect?

Sparrows have small wings and can't fly very fast. So, if a **predator** such as a cat appears, they often run into a bush to hide.

Sparrow fact!
There are different names for sparrows in different parts of the UK. In the north-east of England, they're sometimes called spuggies, spaggies or spadgers.

No other birds live in more places around the world than sparrows. They can live everywhere except freezing-cold Antarctica!

BIRDS OF PREY

Even in the middle of a city, you might be lucky enough to see a powerful natural predator. Look up high for birds of prey like falcons and hawks.

Falcons live on tall buildings in cities including London, Nottingham and Sheffield.

Sparrowhawks are small predators. As their name suggests, they eat little birds like sparrows.

BONUS

THE CROW FAMILY

Here are the five most common sorts of crow living in the UK.

CARRION CROWS

These crows eat carrion (dead animals) as well as things like insects, eggs and fruit. They're black all over. Their call sounds a bit like "caw".

RAVENS

Ravens are the largest birds in the crow family. They have shiny black feathers, and their call sounds like "kronk-kronk-kronk"!

JACKDAWS

Jackdaws are black, with dark grey feathers on their heads and necks. Their call sounds like "jack" or "chack".

MAGPIES

There's no mistaking magpies with their striking black and white bodies and blue wing feathers! They have many calls but a common one sounds like "chak-chak-chak-chak-chak-chak"!

ROOKS

Rooks look a lot like carrion crows, but their large beaks are grey. Their call sounds like "graah-graah".

CHAPTER 3
MINIBEASTS

If you want to spot birds in the city, you need to look up. But lots of amazing creatures are easier to spot by looking down.

Cities are full of fascinating and varied minibeasts. You might spot ants bustling from a crack in the ground. You might notice a slug slithering towards a dandelion on the pavement, or a ladybird on a nettle leaf. Look down and you'll soon discover a minibeast near your feet!

ANTS

There are over 50 different kinds of ants in the UK! However, in town, you're most likely to spot the most common one, the black ant.

Black ants like living outdoors, in grass or under pavements. But they often come into houses in search of food. They don't cause serious damage, but they can spoil food if they climb over it. That's because they may have dirt or bacteria on their feet.

In the garden, black ants are useful to humans! They burrow through soil and mix it up, and they add nutrients to it. This helps plants grow better.

On hot summer days, you might see ants swarming. The queens from lots of ant **colonies** fly into the air and mate with the males. Then the queens burrow back down into the ground to lay their eggs.

Ant fact!
Most of the ants we see are female worker ants. They work hard foraging for food, but they can't lay eggs. Only the queen ant can do this.

SLUGS

Slugs are some of the easiest creatures to spot, even in the middle of town. You often see them when it's been raining.

Slugs breathe through this.

Slugs' bodies are very different from ours. For one thing, slugs' poo comes out of a hole near the side of their head. They have another hole nearby to breathe through.

Slugs don't have legs – but they do have a foot! That's the name for the underside of a slug. Slugs move by tightening and loosening the muscles along their foot, in a rhythmic wave.

Slugs make trails of slime, called mucus. This helps them slide along, and it also helps them to stick to walls and slopes. It guards slugs against drying out, too.

Slug fact!
Slug mucus inspired scientists to invent a new kind of glue! It's used to keep wounds closed after operations.

LADYBIRDS

The ladybird you're most likely to see is the black and red seven-spot ladybird. Other sorts of ladybirds have different numbers of spots, or no spots at all!

The ladybird's bright colours warn other animals – *don't eat me, I taste disgusting!*

Ladybird fact!
When they're threatened, ladybirds squirt a horrible-tasting yellow liquid from their legs. This persuades most predators not to eat them.

A baby ladybird is called a larva. These look nothing like their parents – in fact, they look a bit like tiny alligators!

ladybird larva

BONUS: MINIBEASTS AND NOT-SO-MINI BEASTS

REDBACK SPIDERS

Redback spiders live in many towns in Australia. The female spiders have a bite that can make people ill. Luckily, it's easy to treat with a special substance called antivenom.

GIANT CENTIPEDES

These massive centipedes can be found in South America, Australia, the Caribbean and Hong Kong. They sometimes come indoors to find food or warmth.

GIANT AFRICAN LAND SNAILS

These enormous snails are probably too big to qualify as minibeasts! They have caused problems in towns in Florida, USA. They can carry diseases, and because they're so large, they can also quickly damage crops.

CHAPTER 4
PLANTS

Many cities have parks with glorious displays of plants and flowers. These often change throughout the year to follow the rhythm of the seasons. But it can feel like there's not much growing space in cities for wild plants.

Seaton Park, Aberdeen, Scotland

Actually, if you look carefully, there are wild plants growing almost everywhere. Some are so familiar that we hardly notice them. But even the most common plants are fascinating if you know a bit about them.

DANDELIONS

You'll often see sunshine-yellow dandelion flowers growing in grass verges, or even in pavement cracks or between kerbstones! Look closely, and you'll see they're beautiful – but did you know they're useful, too?

We depend on **pollinating** insects like bees to help our food plants grow. But bee numbers are going down, partly because there's less food for them. Dandelions are important because they're a brilliant source of food for bees.

Each dandelion flower is actually made up of many tiny flowers packed together.

Each tiny flower has a store of sweet nectar inside, which bees love. This helps keep the bees' energy up in early spring, before most other flowers have appeared.

We can eat dandelions, too. The leaves are used in salads, and some people make tea from the flowers!

Warning! Always check with a grown-up before eating any wild plant!

Dandelion fact!
The dandelion's name comes from the French for "lion's teeth", because of its jagged leaves.

IVY

You've probably seen **evergreen** ivy growing on walls, trees and fences. It can grow anywhere, even in the noisiest, most crowded city centre!

Some people worry that ivy will kill trees or damage buildings. But that's far from true! Ivy helps to keep buildings cooler in summer and warmer in winter. It won't damage a building unless the walls are already crumbly. And ivy leaves even help us breathe more easily, by taking **pollutants** out of the air.

Bees and other pollinators love ivy flowers! These bloom in autumn, when fewer other flowers are around. This makes them a fantastic food source for insects at a time when other food is scarce.

Ivy fact!

Ivy berries are crucial food for birds in autumn and winter. They're packed with fats and nutrients – like a bird energy bar!

NETTLES

Nettles grow on overlooked patches of land, from road verges to car parks. If you've ever been stung by a nettle, you'll know one important thing about this underrated plant!

Nettle stings aren't much fun, but lots of wild creatures depend on nettles.

The caterpillars of red admiral and peacock butterflies munch on the leaves. Ladybirds love nettles too, because they're full of the food ladybirds like best – **aphids**.

peacock butterfly caterpillar

Nettle fact!

Nettles are edible. You can't eat them raw, but they make a tasty soup. People sometimes use them to colour clothes, too. They make material turn dark green!

BONUS

AMAZING CITY NATURE PROJECTS

This tower block in Milan, Italy, is called the "vertical wood". It's covered in trees and shrubs which attract 1,600 different **species** of birds and butterflies!

The city of Berlin in Germany is creating more than 50 wildflower meadows and gardens. They aim to provide food and shelter for some of the 300 different local species of wild bees.

CHAPTER 5
HIDDEN NATURE

Living things are all around us in cities and towns, but sometimes you have to look hard to spot them. One interesting place to look for tiny plants and animals is in a crack in a wall or pavement. Take a closer look at cracks and crevices – you never know what you might find!

Warning!
Stay safe when nature-spotting near roads. Don't step off the pavement, and watch out for vehicles and other pedestrians!

PAVEMENT PLANTS

Here are just some of the hundreds of different tiny plants that can live in pavement or wall cracks.

Speedwell

These tiny blue flowers were once used to help heal wounds. Their name might come from the fact that they gave people a "speedy" recovery!

Herb-robert

Long ago, this plant was used to stop nosebleeds and stomach upsets. Sometimes people carried it for good luck.

Scarlet pimpernel

This flower is also called
"shepherd's weather-glass", because
some people believe it can help
predict the weather.
It closes up when storms
are coming!

Chickweed

This flower got its name
because people used to feed it
to chickens! Some people eat it,
too, in salads.

CREATURES IN THE CRACKS

Woodlice

You might find a woodlouse living in a crack in the pavement or wall. They like to stay damp, so they hide away from the sunlight.

They're sometimes called "pill bugs", because when they're threatened, they roll up into a ball that looks like a pill.

Woodlouse spiders

As you can probably guess, these spiders like to eat woodlice. They also like living in cracks. They've got strong jaws that could bite you if you get too close! Their bite might hurt a little, but it's not dangerous.

Hibernating ladybirds

If you're lucky, in autumn or winter you might even see lots of ladybirds **hibernating** together in a crack!

AFTER DARK

Some fascinating city animals are tricky to spot because they don't come out in daylight.

Bats

Bats live in many towns and cities. There may well be some living near you, even if you've never seen them! They like to **roost** in cracks and crevices in old buildings, or under bridges.

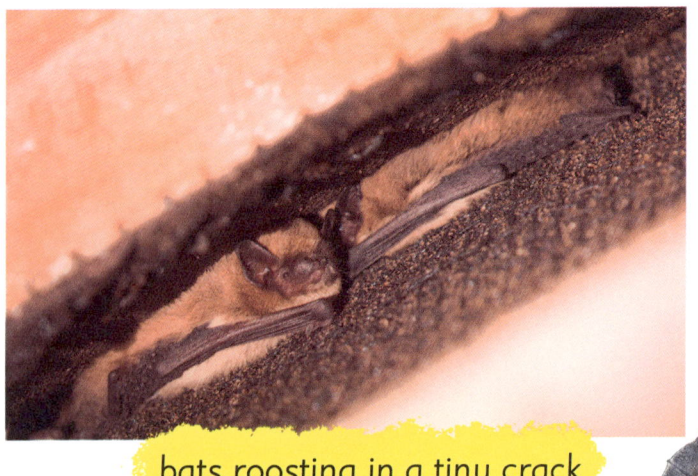

bats roosting in a tiny crack

For the best chance of seeing bats, go out at dusk. You might see them flying near a pond, lake or river. They swoop low over the water, looking for insects to eat.

Hedgehogs

Hedgehogs are much rarer than they used to be. However, you still might be lucky enough to see one snuffling around a garden or trundling along the street after dark.

Curiously, hedgehogs seem to be doing better in towns and cities than in the countryside. That's because more people are making parks and gardens hedgehog-friendly. This means leaving holes in fences for hedgehogs to travel through, and leaving some areas of the garden a bit untidy! Hedgehogs like to live quietly in overgrown areas.

CHAPTER 6
INVITING NATURE IN

We've already seen there are lots of wild plants and animals living in cities. But in many urban areas, people are trying to create even more space for nature. There are plenty of reasons why.

First of all – humans are animals too! We're part of nature, not apart from it. The more connected to nature we are, the better we'll look after the world around us.

pond-dipping in London

Researchers have found that when people have access to nature, they enjoy life more. Experiencing nature boosts our mood and helps our **mental** health. Walking, running and playing outside improves our **physical** health, too. And obviously, all kinds of wild creatures thrive in green spaces.

Here are some of the ways people are bringing more nature into towns and cities.

TINY FORESTS

Around the UK, people are planting tiny forests in the heart of cities! Each tiny forest has about 600 trees planted closely together in an area the size of a tennis court. Lots of urban schools and businesses are planting these rich little patches of woodland.

Although these forests are small, they are incredibly effective! Within three years of planting, around 500 different species of plants and animals typically live in a tiny forest.

LIVING WALLS AND GREEN ROOFS

Some city buildings are literally covered in plants! Living walls and green roofs help attract pollinators. The plants also reduce air pollution by absorbing tiny polluting **particles** through their leaves.

Over 8,000 plants from 21 different species are sharing this living wall in Covent Garden, London. It includes a special system to water the plants with rainwater!

Green roofs can be enormous or tiny. The top of this shed is covered in varied plants and fungi.

This green roof in London has plenty of room for plants and people!

A shopping centre in Liverpool has a living wall 65 metres long – and two beehives on the roof. The bees pollinate the plants in the living wall. Plants up to five kilometres away receive visits from them, too. In their first year, the bees produced 180 jars of honey!

HOW CAN YOU HELP?

If you have a garden or balcony, you could plant pollinator-friendly flowers like lavender in a pot. You could hang up a bird feeder, or make a bug hotel from sticks and junk materials.

But not everyone has access to outdoor space. If you don't, you can still help!

One of the best things you can do to help nature is keep your eyes open. Look out for plants and animals at the bus stop or on the way to school.

If you see something interesting, show it to other people. You might persuade them to look out for nature, too! The more we all know about nature, the easier it will be for us to take care of it, and enjoy it too.

GLOSSARY

aphids tiny insects that damage plants

colonies groups of animals living together

evergreen plants with leaves that stay green all year

hibernating sleeping all through the winter

mental to do with the mind

nutrients the things in food that help to keep plants and animals healthy

particles tiny pieces, often too small to see

physical to do with the body

pollinating transferring pollen from one plant to another, so plants can produce fruit and seeds

pollutants things that cause pollution by making the air, land or water dirty or unsafe

predator an animal that hunts and eats other animals

roost shelter and sleep

species a particular kind of plant or animal

urban living in a city or to do with cities

About the author

Why did you want to write this book?

Catherine Baker

As a child, I lived on the outskirts of London. I didn't really notice the plants and animals living around me. I used to think nature was something you could only see by visiting the countryside. Looking back, I think that was a shame! There are so many fascinating plants and animals living in towns and cities, but somehow I didn't really value them. I wrote this book to draw attention to the beautiful wild plants and creatures that are all around us, wherever we live!

What was the most interesting thing you learnt while writing this book?

Before I started working on the book, I seldom thought about slugs. But now I'm a bit obsessed with them! The fact about slugs that I love best is that their poo comes out of a hole near the side of their head. Also, did you know that slugs are right-handed? OK, they don't actually have hands – but their breathing hole and most of their organs are on the right-hand side of their bodies. I'd love to write a book that's all about slugs one day – they're amazing!

How did you go about writing a non-fiction book like this?
First I read lots of books about urban wildlife. Then I spent hours on the internet looking up unusual facts about common plants and animals. I ended up with FAR more information than I could possibly use in this book! The tricky bit was trying to decide what to include, and what to leave out.

What sort of urban wild animal do you like best?
It's really hard to choose, because they're all fascinating. But if I have to pick one, I'll go for hedgehogs. I'm lucky because hedgehogs sometimes visit my garden. They're such shy creatures that I don't often see them, but when I do, it's always a lovely moment!

What do you hope readers will get from this book?
I really hope it will encourage readers to keep an eye open for interesting plants and animals living near them. There are so many wonderful creatures to spot, even in a city centre! Once you start looking, you'll see more and more.

What urban animal or plant would you love to see?
Did you know that seals and dolphins are sometimes spotted in the big river that runs through London? I would be so excited to see one of those beautiful creatures swimming in the river. I'll have to keep my eyes open – maybe one day I will!

Book chat

When you looked at the cover of the book, what did you think it would be about? Did you change your mind as you read it?

Have you seen any plants or animals from this book near where you live?

Which of the creatures in the book would you most like to spot?

What is the most unusual fact you learnt from reading this book?

If you could add one plant or animal that you know to this book, which would you add?

Did anything really surprise you in this book?

Would you recommend this book? Why, or why not?

What part of the book did you like best, and why?

If you could give the author one piece of advice about this book, what would you say?

Which plant or animal from the book would you like to find out more about?

If you had to think of a new title for the book, what would you choose?

If you had to give the book a three-word review, what would you say?

Book challenge:

Go for a walk near where you live. How many different wild plants and animals can you spot?

Published by Collins An imprint of HarperCollins*Publishers*

The News Building
1 London Bridge Street
London
SE1 9GF
UK

Macken House
39/40 Mayor Street Upper
Dublin 1
D01 C9W8
Ireland

© HarperCollins*Publishers* Limited 2025

10 9 8 7 6 5 4 3 2

ISBN 978-0-00-874631-5

All rights reserved. No part of this publication may be reproduced, stored in a retrieval system, or transmitted in any form by any means, electronic, mechanical, photocopying, recording or otherwise, without the prior written permission of the Publisher or a licence permitting restricted copying in the United Kingdom issued by the Copyright Licensing Agency Ltd, 5th Floor, Shackleton House, 4 Battle Bridge Lane, London SE1 2HX.

Without limiting the author's and publisher's exclusive rights, any unauthorised use of this publication to train generative artificial intelligence (AI) technologies is expressly prohibited. HarperCollins also exercise their rights under Article 4(3) of the Digital Single Market Directive 2019/790 and expressly reserve this publication from the text and data mining exception.

British Library Cataloguing-in-Publication Data
A catalogue record for this publication is available from the British Library.

Download the teaching notes and word cards to accompany this book at:
http://littlewandle.org.uk/signupfluency/

Get the latest Collins Big Cat news at
collins.co.uk/collinsbigcat

Author: Catherine Baker
Publisher: Laura White
Product managers: Caroline Green
and Holly Woolnough
Series editor: Charlotte Raby
Phonics consultant: Catherine Baker
Commissioning editor
and project manager: Emily Hooton
Copyeditor: Sally Byford
Proofreader: Catherine Dakin
Cover designer: Sarah Finan
Typesetter: 2Hoots Publishing Services Ltd
Production controller: Katharine Willard

Printed in the UK.

 MIX
Paper | Supporting
responsible forestry
FSC
www.fsc.org **FSC™ C007454**

This book contains FSC™ certified paper and other controlled sources to ensure responsible forest management.

For more information visit: www.harpercollins.co.uk/green

Made with responsibly sourced paper and vegetable ink

Scan to see how we are reducing our environmental impact.

Acknowledgements
The publishers gratefully acknowledge the permission granted to reproduce the copyright material in this book. Every effort has been made to trace copyright holders and to obtain their permission for the use of copyright material. The publishers will gladly receive any information enabling them to rectify any error or omission at the first opportunity.

Front cover beeboys/Shutterstock, back cover tl IrinaK/Shutterstock, tr asharkyu/Shutterstock, bl Drakuliren/Shutterstock, br Eric Isselee/Shutterstock p4b Danielle Connor/Alamy, p5 PhotoStock-Israel/Alamy, pp6–7 Oliver Smart/Alamy, p10 Tim Graham/Getty Images, p23t Nature Picture Library/Alamy, p23b Wildlife World/Alamy, p29 Nature Picture Library/Alamy, p34 Dorling Kindersley Ltd/Alamy, pp36–37b Scenics & Science/Alamy, p38 Simon Price/Alamy, p45b imageBROKER.com GmbH & Co. KG/Alamy, p47 Agencja Fotograficzna Caro/Alamy, pp48–49 Charles Stirling/Alamy, p54c David Chapman/Alamy, p55b Nature Picture Library/Alamy, p57 BSIP SA/Alamy, p59 Joe Blossom/Alamy, pp64–65 Pat Tuson/Alamy.

All other photos Shutterstock.